San
Favorite Cookies
Sweet Treats for the Christmas Season

D0462994

Candy Cane Cookies

1 cup sugar
⅔ cup FLEISCHMANN'S® Original Margarine, softened
½ cup EGG BEATERS® Healthy Real Egg Substitute
2 teaspoons vanilla extract
1 teaspoon almond extract
3 cups all-purpose flour
1 teaspoon DAVIS® Baking Powder
½ teaspoon red food coloring

1. Beat sugar and margarine in large bowl with mixer at medium speed until creamy. Beat in egg substitute, vanilla and almond extracts. Mix flour and baking powder; stir into margarine mixture.

2. Divide dough in half; tint half with red food coloring. Wrap each half and refrigerate at least 2 hours.

3. Divide each half into 32 pieces. Roll each piece into a 5-inch rope. Twist 1 red and 1 white rope together; bend 1 end to form candy cane shape. Place on ungreased baking sheets.

4. Bake in preheated 350°F oven for 8 to 10 minutes or just until set and lightly golden. Remove from sheets; cool on wire racks. Store in airtight container.

Makes 32 cookies

Decadent Brownies

½ cup dark corn syrup
½ cup butter or margarine
6 squares (1 ounce *each*) semisweet chocolate
¾ cup sugar
3 eggs
1 cup all-purpose flour
1 cup chopped walnuts
1 teaspoon vanilla
Fudge Glaze (recipe follows)

Preheat oven to 350°F. Grease 8-inch square pan. Combine corn syrup, butter and chocolate in large heavy saucepan. Place over low heat; stir until chocolate is melted and ingredients are blended. Remove from heat; blend in sugar. Stir in eggs, flour, chopped walnuts and vanilla. Spread batter evenly in prepared pan. Bake 20 to 25 minutes or just until center is set. *Do not overbake.* Meanwhile, prepare Fudge Glaze. Remove brownies from oven. Immediately spread glaze evenly over hot brownies. Cool in pan on wire rack. Cut into 2-inch squares.

Makes 16 brownies

Fudge Glaze

3 squares (1 ounce *each*) semisweet chocolate
2 tablespoons dark corn syrup
1 tablespoon butter or margarine
1 teaspoon light cream or milk

Combine chocolate, corn syrup and butter in small heavy saucepan. Stir over low heat until smooth; add cream.

Candy Cane Cookies

Festive Fudge Blossoms

¼ cup butter or margarine, softened
1 box (18.25 ounces) chocolate
    fudge cake mix
1 egg, lightly beaten
¾ to 1 cup finely chopped walnuts
48 chocolate star candies

Preheat oven to 350°F. Cut butter into cake mix in large bowl until coarse crumbs form. Stir in egg and 2 tablespoons water until well blended. Shape dough into ½-inch balls; roll in walnuts, pressing nuts gently into dough. Place about 2 inches apart onto ungreased baking sheets. Bake cookies 12 minutes or until puffed and nearly set. Place chocolate star in center of each cookie; bake 1 minute. Cool 2 minutes on baking sheet. Remove cookies from baking sheets to wire racks to cool completely.

Makes 4 dozen cookies

Helpful Hint

Chocolate should be stored in a cool, dry place (60°F to 70°F) to avoid the appearance of "bloom," a gray-white film on the surface.

Fruitcake Slices

1 cup butter or margarine, softened
1 cup powdered sugar
1 egg
1 teaspoon vanilla extract
1½ cups coarsely chopped candied
    fruit (fruitcake mix)
½ cup coarsely chopped walnuts
2½ cups all-purpose unsifted flour,
    divided
¾ to 1 cup flaked coconut

Beat butter in large bowl with electric mixer at medium speed until smooth. Add powdered sugar; beat until well blended. Add egg and vanilla; beat until well blended.

Combine candied fruit and walnuts in medium bowl. Stir ¼ cup flour into fruit mixture. Add remaining 2¼ cups flour to butter mixture; beat at low speed until blended. Stir in fruit mixture with spoon.

Shape dough into 2 logs, each about 2 inches in diameter and 5½ inches long. Spread coconut evenly on sheet of waxed paper. Roll logs in coconut, coating evenly. Wrap each log in plastic wrap. Refrigerate 2 to 3 hours or overnight, or freeze up to 1 month. (Let frozen logs stand at room temperature about 10 minutes before slicing and baking.)

Preheat oven to 350°F. Grease cookie sheets. Cut logs into ¼-inch-thick slices; place 1 inch apart on cookie sheets.

Bake 13 to 15 minutes or until edges are golden brown. Transfer to wire racks to cool.   *Makes about 4 dozen cookies*

Festive Fudge Blossoms

Linzer Sandwich Cookies

1⅓ cups all-purpose flour
¼ teaspoon baking powder
¼ teaspoon salt
¾ cup granulated sugar
½ cup butter, softened
1 egg
1 teaspoon vanilla
  Powdered sugar (optional)
  Seedless raspberry jam

Combine flour, baking powder and salt in small bowl. Beat granulated sugar and butter in medium bowl with electric mixer at medium speed until light and fluffy. Beat in egg and vanilla. Gradually add flour mixture. Beat at low speed until dough forms. Divide dough in half; cover and refrigerate 2 hours or until firm.

Preheat oven to 375°F. Working with 1 portion at a time, roll out dough on lightly floured surface to ³⁄₁₆-inch thickness. Cut dough into desired shapes with floured cookie cutters. Cut out equal numbers of each shape. (If dough becomes too soft, refrigerate several minutes before continuing.) Cut 1-inch centers out of half the cookies of each shape. Reroll trimmings and cut out more cookies. Place cookies 1½ to 2 inches apart on ungreased cookie sheets. Bake 7 to 9 minutes or until edges are lightly brown. Let cookies stand on cookie sheets 1 to 2 minutes. Remove cookies to wire racks; cool completely.

Sprinkle cookies with holes with powdered sugar, if desired. Spread 1 teaspoon jam on flat side of whole cookies, spreading almost to edges. Place cookies with holes, flat side down, over jam to create sandwich.
Makes about 2 dozen cookies

Peanut Butter Chocolate Chippers

1 cup creamy peanut butter
1 cup packed light brown sugar
1 egg
¾ cup milk chocolate chips
  Granulated sugar

Preheat oven to 350°F. Combine peanut butter, sugar and egg in medium bowl; mix with spoon. Add chips; mix well. Roll heaping tablespoonfuls of dough into 1½-inch balls. Place balls 2 inches apart on ungreased cookie sheets. Dip fork into granulated sugar; press criss-cross fashion onto each ball, flattening to ½-inch thickness. Bake 12 minutes or until set. Let cookies stand on cookie sheets 2 minutes. Remove cookies with spatula to wire racks; cool completely
Makes about 2 dozen cookies

Note: This simple recipe is unusual because it doesn't contain any flour—but it still makes great cookies!

Linzer Sandwich Cookies

Almond Milk Chocolate Chippers

½ cup slivered almonds
1¼ cups all-purpose flour
½ teaspoon baking soda
½ teaspoon salt
½ cup butter or margarine, softened
½ cup firmly packed light brown
    sugar
⅓ cup granulated sugar
1 egg
2 tablespoons almond-flavored
    liqueur
1 cup milk chocolate chips

1. Preheat oven to 350°F. To toast almonds, spread on baking sheet. Bake 8 to 10 minutes or until golden brown, stirring frequently. Remove almonds from pan and cool; set aside.

2. *Increase oven temperature to 375°F.* Place flour, baking soda and salt in small bowl; stir to combine.

3. Beat butter, brown sugar and granulated sugar in large bowl with electric mixer at medium speed until light and fluffy. Beat in egg until well blended. Beat in liqueur. Gradually add flour mixture. Beat at low speed until well blended. Stir in chips and almonds with spoon.

4. Drop rounded teaspoonfuls of dough 2 inches apart onto ungreased cookie sheets.

5. Bake 9 to 10 minutes or until edges are golden brown. Let cookies stand on cookie sheets 2 minutes. Remove cookies with spatula to wire racks; cool completely.
Makes about 3 dozen cookies

Frosty's Colorful Cookies

1¼ cups firmly packed light brown
    sugar
¾ Butter Flavor* CRISCO® Stick or
    ¾ cup Butter Flavor CRISCO
    all-vegetable shortening
2 tablespoons milk
1 tablespoon vanilla
1 egg
1¾ cups all-purpose flour
1 teaspoon salt
¾ teaspoon baking soda
2 cups red and green candy-coated
    chocolate pieces

*Butter Flavor Crisco® is artificially flavored.

1. Heat oven to 375°F. Place sheets of foil on countertop for cooling cookies.

2. Place brown sugar, ¾ cup shortening, milk and vanilla in large bowl. Beat at medium speed of electric mixer until well blended. Add egg; beat well.

3. Combine flour, salt and baking soda. Add to shortening mixture; beat at low speed just until blended. Stir in candy-coated chocolate pieces.

4. Drop dough by rounded measuring tablespoonfuls 3 inches apart onto ungreased baking sheets.

5. Bake one baking sheet at a time at 375°F for 8 to 10 minutes for chewy cookies, or 11 to 13 minutes for crisp cookies. *Do not overbake.* Cool 2 minutes on baking sheet. Remove cookies to foil to cool completely.
Makes about 3 dozen cookies

Almond Milk Chocolate Chippers

Yuletide Linzer Bars

1⅓ cups butter or margarine,
    softened
¾ cup sugar
1 egg
1 teaspoon grated lemon peel
2½ cups all-purpose flour
1½ cups whole almonds, ground
1 teaspoon ground cinnamon
¾ cup raspberry preserves
    Powdered sugar

Preheat oven to 350°F. Grease
13×9-inch baking pan.

Beat butter and sugar in large bowl with
electric mixer until creamy. Beat in egg
and lemon peel until blended. Mix in flour,
almonds and cinnamon until well blended.

Press 2 cups dough into bottom of
prepared pan. Spread preserves over
crust. Press remaining dough, a small
amount at a time, evenly over preserves.

Bake 35 to 40 minutes until golden
brown. Cool in pan on wire rack. Sprinkle
with powdered sugar; cut into bars.

Makes 36 bars

Oatmeal Raisin Cookies

¾ cup all-purpose flour
¾ teaspoon salt
½ teaspoon baking soda
½ teaspoon ground cinnamon
¾ cup butter or margarine, softened
¾ cup granulated sugar
¾ cup packed light brown sugar
1 egg
1 tablespoon water
3 teaspoons vanilla, divided
3 cups uncooked quick-cooking or
    old-fashioned oats
1 cup raisins
½ cup powdered sugar
1 tablespoon milk

Preheat oven to 375°F. Grease cookie
sheets; set aside. Combine flour, salt,
baking soda and cinnamon in small bowl.

Beat butter, granulated sugar and brown
sugar in large bowl with electric mixer at
medium speed until light and fluffy. Add
egg, water and 2 teaspoons vanilla; beat
well. Add flour mixture; beat at low speed
just until blended. Stir in oats with spoon.
Stir in raisins.

Drop tablespoonfuls of dough 2 inches
apart onto prepared cookie sheets.

Bake 10 to 11 minutes or until edges
are golden brown. Let cookies stand
2 minutes on cookie sheets; transfer
to wire racks to cool completely.

For glaze, stir powdered sugar, milk and
remaining 1 teaspoon vanilla in small
bowl until smooth. Drizzle over cookies
with fork or spoon.

Makes about 4 dozen cookies

Yuletide Linzer Bars

Jolly Peanut Butter Gingerbread Cookies

1⅔ cups (10-ounce package)
   REESE'S® Peanut Butter Chips
¾ cup (1½ sticks) butter, softened
1 cup packed light brown sugar
1 cup dark corn syrup
2 eggs
5 cups all-purpose flour
1 teaspoon baking soda
½ teaspoon ground cinnamon
¼ teaspoon ground ginger
¼ teaspoon salt

1. Place peanut butter chips in small microwave-safe bowl. Microwave at HIGH (100%) 1 to 2 minutes or until chips are melted when stirred. Beat melted peanut butter chips and butter in large bowl until well blended. Add sugar, corn syrup and eggs; beat until light and fluffy. Stir together flour, baking soda, cinnamon, ginger and salt. Add half of flour mixture to butter mixture; beat at low speed of electric mixer until smooth. Stir in remaining flour mixture with spoon until well blended. Divide into thirds; wrap each in plastic wrap. Refrigerate at least 1 hour or until dough is firm enough to roll.

2. Heat oven to 325°F.

3. Roll 1 dough portion at a time to ⅛-inch thickness on lightly floured surface. Cut into holiday shapes with floured cookie cutters. Place on ungreased cookie sheet.

4. Bake 10 to 12 minutes or until set and lightly browned. Cool slightly; remove from cookie sheet to wire rack. Cool completely. Frost and decorate as desired.
Makes about 6 dozen cookies

Luscious Lemon Bars

   Grated peel from 2 lemons
2 cups all-purpose flour
1 cup butter
½ cup powdered sugar
¼ teaspoon salt
1 cup granulated sugar
3 eggs
⅓ cup fresh lemon juice
   Powdered sugar

1. Preheat oven to 350°F. Grease 13×9-inch baking pan; set aside. Place 1 teaspoon lemon peel, flour, butter, powdered sugar and salt in food processor. Process until mixture forms coarse crumbs.

2. Press mixture evenly into prepared 13×9-inch baking pan. Bake 18 to 20 minutes or until golden brown.

3. Beat 3 teaspoons lemon peel, granulated sugar, eggs and lemon juice in medium bowl with electric mixer at medium speed until well blended.

4. Pour mixture evenly over warm crust. Return to oven; bake 18 to 20 minutes or until center is set and edges are golden brown. Remove pan to wire rack; cool completely.

5. Dust with powdered sugar; cut into 2×1½-inch bars. Do not freeze.
Makes 3 dozen bars

Jolly Peanut Butter
Gingerbread Cookies

Christmas Cookie Pops

1 package (20 ounces) refrigerated
  sugar cookie dough
All-purpose flour (optional)
20 to 24 (4-inch) lollipop sticks
Royal Icing (recipe follows)
6 ounces almond bark (vanilla or
  chocolate), or butterscotch
  chips
Vegetable shortening
Assorted small candies

1. Preheat oven to 350°F. Grease cookie sheets; set aside.

2. Remove dough from wrapper according to package directions.

3. Sprinkle dough with flour to minimize sticking, if necessary. Cut dough in half. Reserve 1 half; refrigerate remaining dough.

4. Roll reserved dough to ⅓-inch thickness. Cut out cookies using 3¼- or 3½-inch Christmas cookie cutters. Place lollipop sticks on cookies so that tips of sticks are imbedded in cookies. Carefully turn cookies with spatula so sticks are in back; place on prepared cookie sheets. Repeat with remaining dough.

5. Bake 7 to 11 minutes or until edges are lightly browned. Cool cookies on sheets 2 minutes. Remove cookies to wire racks; cool completely.

6. Prepare Royal Icing.

7. Melt almond bark in medium microwavable bowl according to package directions. Add 1 or more tablespoons shortening if coating is too thick. Hold cookies over bowl; spoon coating over cookies. Scrape excess coating from cookie edges. Decorate with Royal Icing and small candies immediately. Place cookies on wire racks set over waxed paper; let dry.

Makes 20 to 24 cookies

Royal Icing

2 to 3 egg whites
2 to 4 cups powdered sugar
1 tablespoon lemon juice
Liquid food coloring (optional)

Beat 2 egg whites in medium bowl with electric mixer until peaks just begin to hold their shape. Add 2 cups sugar and lemon juice; beat for 1 minute. If consistency is too thin for piping, gradually add more sugar until desired result is achieved; if it is too thick, add another egg white. Divide icing among several small bowls and tint to desired colors. Keep bowls tightly covered until ready to use.

Helpful Hint

When rolling out cookie dough, work with small amounts and keep the remaining dough covered with plastic wrap to prevent it from drying out.

Rum Fruitcake Cookies

1 cup sugar
¾ cup vegetable shortening
3 eggs
⅓ cup orange juice
1 tablespoon rum extract
3 cups all-purpose flour
2 teaspoons baking powder
1 teaspoon baking soda
1 teaspoon salt
2 cups (8 ounces) candied fruit
1 cup raisins
1 cup nuts, coarsely chopped

1. Preheat oven to 375°F. Lightly grease cookie sheets; set aside. Beat sugar and shortening in large bowl until fluffy. Add eggs, orange juice and rum extract; beat 2 minutes longer.

2. Combine flour, baking powder, baking soda and salt in small bowl. Add fruit, raisins and nuts. Stir into creamed mixture. Drop dough by rounded teaspoonfuls 2 inches apart onto prepared cookie sheets. Bake 10 to 12 minutes or until golden. Let cookies stand on cookie sheets 2 minutes. Remove to wire rack; cool completely.

Makes about 6 dozen cookies

Holiday Wreath Cookies

1 package (20 ounces) refrigerated sugar cookie dough
2 cups shredded coconut
2 to 3 drops green food color
1 container (16 ounces) ready-to-spread French vanilla frosting
Green sugar or small cinnamon candies

1. Preheat oven to 350°F. Divide cookie dough in half (keep half of dough refrigerated until needed). Roll dough out on well-floured surface to ⅛-inch-thick rectangle. Cut with cookie cutters to resemble wreaths. Repeat with remaining half of dough.

2. Place cookies about 2 inches apart on ungreased baking sheets. Bake 7 to 9 minutes or until edges are lightly browned. Remove cookies from baking sheets to wire rack to cool completely.

3. Place coconut in resealable plastic food storage bag. Add food color; seal bag and shake until coconut is evenly colored. Frost cookies with frosting and decorate with coconut or green sugar and cinnamon candies.

Makes about 2 dozen cookies

Rum Fruitcake Cookies

Christmas Tree Platter

**Christmas Ornament Cookie
Dough (recipe follows)
2 cups sifted powdered sugar
2 tablespoons milk or lemon juice
Assorted food colors, colored
    sugars and assorted small
    decors**

1. Prepare Christmas Ornament Cookie Dough. Divide dough in half. Reserve 1 half; refrigerate remaining dough. Roll reserved half of dough to ⅛-inch thickness.

2. Preheat oven to 350°F. Cut out tree shapes with cookie cutters. Place on ungreased cookie sheets.

3. Bake 10 to 12 minutes or until edges are lightly browned. Remove to wire racks; cool completely.

4. Repeat with remaining half of dough. Reroll scraps; cut into small circles for ornaments, squares and rectangles for gift boxes and tree trunks.

5. Bake 8 to 12 minutes, depending on size of cookies.

6. Mix powdered sugar and milk for icing. Tint most of icing green and a smaller amount red or other colors for ornaments and boxes. Spread green icing on trees. Sprinkle ornaments and boxes with colored sugars or decorate as desired.

7. Arrange cookies on flat platter to resemble tree as shown in photo.
Makes about 1 dozen cookies

Christmas Ornament Cookie Dough

**2¼ cups all-purpose flour
  ¼ teaspoon salt
  1 cup granulated sugar
  ¾ cup butter or margarine, softened
  1 egg
  1 teaspoon vanilla
  1 teaspoon almond extract**

Combine flour and salt in medium bowl. Beat sugar and butter in large bowl at medium speed of electric mixer until fluffy. Beat in egg, vanilla and almond extract. Gradually add flour mixture. Beat at low speed until well blended. Form dough into 2 discs; wrap in plastic wrap and refrigerate 30 minutes or until firm.

Helpful Hint

Use this beautiful Christmas Tree Platter cookie as your centerpiece for this holiday's family dinner. It is sure to receive lots of "oohs" and "ahs!"

Caramel Fudge Brownies

1 jar (12 ounces) hot caramel ice
   cream topping
1¼ cups all-purpose flour, divided
¼ teaspoon baking powder
   Dash salt
4 squares (1 ounce *each*)
   unsweetened chocolate,
   coarsely chopped
¾ cup butter or margarine
2 cups sugar
3 eggs
2 teaspoons vanilla
¾ cup semisweet chocolate chips
¾ cup chopped pecans

Preheat oven to 350°F. Lightly grease
13×9-inch baking pan.

Combine caramel topping and ¼ cup
flour in small bowl; set aside.

Combine remaining 1 cup flour, baking
powder and salt in small bowl; mix well.

Place unsweetened chocolate squares
and margarine in medium microwavable
bowl. Microwave at HIGH 2 minutes or
until margarine is melted; stir until
chocolate is completely melted.

Stir sugar into melted chocolate with
mixing spoon. Add eggs and vanilla; stir
until combined.

Add flour mixture, stirring until well
blended. Spread chocolate mixture
evenly into prepared pan.

Bake 25 minutes. Immediately after
removing brownies from oven, spread
caramel mixture over brownies. Sprinkle
top evenly with chocolate chips and
pecans.

Return pan to oven; bake 20 to
25 minutes or until topping is golden
brown and bubbling. *Do not overbake.*
Cool brownies completely in pan on wire
rack. Cut into 2×1½-inch bars.
Makes 3 dozen brownies

Thumbprint Cookies

1 cup butter or margarine
¼ cup sugar
1 teaspoon almond extract
2 cups all-purpose flour
½ teaspoon salt
1 cup finely chopped nuts, if desired
   SMUCKER'S® Preserves or Jams
   (any flavor)

Combine butter and sugar; beat until light
and fluffy. Blend in almond extract. Add
flour and salt; mix well.

Shape level tablespoonfuls of dough into
balls; roll in nuts. Place on ungreased
cookie sheets; flatten slightly. Indent
centers; fill with preserves or jams.

Bake at 400°F for 10 to 12 minutes or just
until lightly browned.
Makes 2½ dozen cookies

Caramel Fudge Brownies

Slice 'n' Bake Ginger Wafers

½ cup butter or margarine, softened
1 cup packed brown sugar
¼ cup light molasses
1 egg
2 teaspoons ground ginger
1 teaspoon grated orange peel
¼ teaspoon salt
¼ teaspoon ground cinnamon
¼ teaspoon ground cloves
2 cups all-purpose flour

1. Beat butter, sugar and molasses in large bowl until light and fluffy. Add egg, ginger, orange peel, salt, cinnamon and cloves; beat until well blended. Stir in flour until well blended. (Dough will be very stiff.)

2. Divide dough in half. Roll each half into 8×1½-inch log. Wrap logs in waxed paper or plastic wrap; refrigerate at least 5 hours or up to 3 days.

3. Preheat oven to 350°F. Cut dough into ¼-inch-thick slices. Place about 2 inches apart on ungreased baking sheets. Bake 12 to 14 minutes or until set. Remove from baking sheet to wire rack to cool.
Makes about 4½ dozen cookies

Serving Suggestion: Dip half of each cookie in melted white chocolate or drizzle cookies with a glaze of 1¼ cups powdered sugar and 2 tablespoons orange juice. Or, cut cookie dough into ⅛-inch-thick slices; bake and sandwich melted caramel candy or peanut butter between cookies.

Scrumptious Chocolate Fruit and Nut Cookies

1¼ cups butter or margarine, softened
2 cups sugar
2 eggs
2 teaspoons vanilla extract
2 cups all-purpose flour
¾ cup HERSHEY'S Cocoa
1 teaspoon baking soda
½ teaspoon salt
2 cups (12-ounce package) HERSHEY'S Semi-Sweet Chocolate Chips
1 cup chopped dried apricots
1 cup coarsely chopped macadamia nuts

1. Heat oven to 350°F. Beat butter and sugar in large bowl until light and fluffy. Add eggs and vanilla; beat well. Stir together flour, cocoa, baking soda and salt; blend into butter mixture. Stir in chocolate chips, apricots and nuts.

2. Using ice cream scoop or ¼ cup measuring cup, drop dough onto ungreased cookie sheet.

3. Bake 12 to 14 minutes or until set. Cool slightly; remove from cookie sheet to wire rack. Cool completely.
Makes about 2 dozen (3½ inch) cookies

Slice 'n' Bake Ginger Wafers

Mocha Crinkles

1⅓ cups firmly packed light brown
    sugar
½ cup vegetable oil
¼ cup low-fat sour cream
1 egg
1 teaspoon vanilla
1¾ cups all-purpose flour
¾ cup unsweetened cocoa powder
2 teaspoons instant espresso or
    coffee granules
1 teaspoon baking soda
¼ teaspoon salt
⅛ teaspoon ground black pepper
½ cup powdered sugar

1. Beat brown sugar and oil in medium
bowl with electric mixer. Mix in sour
cream, egg and vanilla. Set aside.

2. Mix flour, cocoa, espresso, baking
soda, salt and pepper in another medium
bowl.

3. Add flour mixture to brown sugar
mixture; mix well. Refrigerate dough until
firm, 3 to 4 hours.

4. Preheat oven to 350°F. Pour powdered
sugar into shallow bowl. Set aside. Cut
dough into 1-inch pieces; roll into balls.
Roll balls in powdered sugar.

5. Bake on ungreased cookie sheets
10 to 12 minutes or until tops of cookies
are firm to touch. *Do not overbake.* Cool
on wire racks.   *Makes 6 dozen cookies*

Peanut Gems

2½ cups all-purpose flour
1 teaspoon baking powder
⅛ teaspoon salt
1 cup butter, softened
1 cup packed light brown sugar
2 eggs
2 teaspoons vanilla
1½ cups cocktail peanuts, finely
    chopped
    Powdered sugar (optional)

Preheat oven to 350°F. Combine flour,
baking powder and salt in small bowl.

Beat butter in large bowl with electric
mixer at medium speed until smooth.
Gradually beat in brown sugar; increase
speed to medium-high and beat until light
and fluffy. Beat in eggs, 1 at a time, until
fluffy. Beat in vanilla. Gradually stir in
flour mixture until blended. Stir in peanuts
until blended.

Drop heaping tablespoonfuls of dough
about 1 inch apart onto ungreased cookie
sheets; flatten slightly with hands.

Bake 12 minutes or until set. Let cookies
stand on cookie sheets 5 minutes; transfer
to wire racks to cool completely. Dust
cookies with powdered sugar, if desired.
Store in airtight container.
    Makes about 2½ dozen cookies

Two-Toned Spritz Cookies

1 square (1 ounce) unsweetened chocolate, coarsely chopped
1 cup (2 sticks) butter or margarine, softened
1 cup sugar
1 egg
1 teaspoon vanilla
2¼ cups all-purpose flour
¼ teaspoon salt

Melt chocolate in small heavy saucepan over low heat, stirring constantly; set aside. Beat butter and sugar in large bowl until light and fluffy. Beat in egg and vanilla. Combine flour and salt in medium bowl; gradually add to butter mixture. Reserve 2 cups dough. Beat chocolate into dough in bowl until smooth. Cover both doughs and refrigerate until firm enough to handle, about 20 minutes.

Preheat oven to 400°F. Roll out vanilla dough between two sheets of waxed paper to ½-inch thickness. Cut into 5×4-inch rectangles. Place chocolate dough on sheet of waxed paper. Using waxed paper to hold dough, roll back and forth to form a log about 1 inch in diameter. Cut into 5-inch-long logs. Place chocolate log in center of vanilla rectangle. Wrap vanilla dough around log and fit into cookie press fitted with star disc. Press dough onto ungreased cookie sheets 1½ inches apart. Bake about 10 minutes or until just set. Remove cookies with spatula to wire racks; cool completely.

Makes about 4 dozen cookies

Holiday Chocolate Shortbread Cookies

1 cup (2 sticks) butter, softened
1¼ cups powdered sugar
1 teaspoon vanilla extract
½ cup HERSHEY'S Dutch Processed Cocoa or HERSHEY'S Cocoa
1¾ cups all-purpose flour
1⅔ cups (10-ounce package) HERSHEY'S Premier White Chips

1. Heat oven to 300°F. Beat butter, powdered sugar and vanilla in large bowl until creamy. Add cocoa; beat until well blended. Gradually add flour; stir well.

2. Roll or pat dough to ¼-inch thickness on lightly floured surface or between 2 pieces of wax paper. Cut into holiday shapes using star, tree, wreath or other cookie cutters. Reroll dough scraps, cutting cookies until dough is used. Place on ungreased cookie sheet.

3. Bake 15 to 20 minutes or just until firm. Immediately place white chips, flat side down, in decorative design on warm cookies. Cool slightly; remove from cookie sheet to wire rack. Cool completely.

Makes about 4½ dozen (2-inch diameter) cookies

Note: For more even baking, place similar shapes and sizes of cookies on same cookie sheet.

Two-Toned Spritz Cookies

Mincemeat Pastries

3½ cups all-purpose flour
¾ cup granulated sugar
½ teaspoon salt
½ cup (1 stick) butter, chilled
8 tablespoons vegetable shortening
1 cup buttermilk
1 cup mincemeat
¼ cup powdered sugar (optional)

1. Combine flour, granulated sugar and salt in large bowl; set aside.

2. Cut butter into 1-inch chunks. Add butter and shortening to flour mixture. Cut in with pastry blender or 2 knives until mixture resembles coarse crumbs. Drizzle buttermilk over top; toss just until mixture comes together into a ball.

3. Turn out dough onto lightly floured work surface; fold in half and flatten to about ½ inch thick. Knead about eight times. Divide dough in half; press each half into ½-inch-thick disk. Wrap in plastic wrap and refrigerate at least 30 minutes.

4. Let dough rest at room temperature 10 minutes. Preheat oven to 350°F. Lightly grease cookie sheets; set aside. Roll one disk of dough into 18×12-inch rectangle on lightly floured work surface. Cut into 24 (3-inch) squares. Place heaping ½ teaspoon mincemeat in center of each square. Fold one corner about ⅔ of the way over the filling; fold opposite corner ⅔ of the way over the filling.

5. Place 2 inches apart on prepared cookie sheets. Repeat with remaining dough.

6. Bake 20 minutes or until lightly browned. Remove cookies to wire rack; cool completely. Sprinkle tops of pastries lightly with powdered sugar, if desired.

Makes 4 dozen cookies

Molasses Spice Cookies

1 cup granulated sugar
¾ cup shortening
¼ cup molasses
1 egg, beaten
2 cups all-purpose flour
2 teaspoons baking soda
1 teaspoon ground cinnamon
1 teaspoon ground cloves
1 teaspoon ground ginger
¼ teaspoon dry mustard
¼ teaspoon salt
½ cup granulated brown sugar

1. Preheat oven to 375°F. Grease cookie sheets; set aside.

2. Beat granulated sugar and shortening about 5 minutes in large bowl until light and fluffy. Add molasses and egg; beat until fluffy.

3. Combine flour, baking soda, cinnamon, cloves, ginger, mustard and salt in medium bowl. Add to shortening mixture; mix until just combined.

4. Place brown sugar in shallow dish. Roll tablespoonfuls of dough into 1-inch balls; roll in sugar to coat. Place 2 inches apart on prepared cookie sheets. Bake 15 minutes or until lightly browned. Let cookies stand on cookie sheets 2 minutes. Remove cookies to wire racks; cool. *Makes about 6 dozen cookies*